[un]ravelling

Sue Nyamnjoh

Langaa Research & Publishing CIG
Mankon, Bamenda

Publisher:
Langaa RPCIG
Langaa Research & Publishing Common Initiative Group
P.O. Box 902 Mankon
Bamenda
North West Region
Cameroon
Langaagrp@gmail.com
www.langaa-rpcig.net

Distributed in and outside N. America by African Books Collective
orders@africanbookscollective.com
www.africanbookscollective.com

ISBN-10: 9956-552-59-3

ISBN-13: 978-9956-552-59-7

© Sue Nyamnjoh 2023

Table of Contents

Part Three

Part Four

Preface

The pleasure of reading poetry is not only in the lyricism but in the depth of its thought provocation with nothing more than minimalistic imagery that conjures a world filled with marvel, beauty, love, dreams, pain, and hurt. Yet, the human strife for completeness to mark an end to the vicissitudes of life proves yet, a Sisyphean task. This concept having coloured popular imagination has not left anthropologists indifferent. To this very last mention, Sue Nyamnjoh, invokes at every verse or line possible in her poetry, the impossibility of total satiation of everything life has in store for humans viz. the good the bad, and the ugly. It is therefore no doubt that the second part of this very terse collection opens with "Lost Fruit". The first line is tellingly Nyamnjohian as the poet echoes the concept of a fruit lost only to a new beginning. She writes, "The apple doesn't fall far from the tree". A fruit falling by the tree only so does to guarantee continuity and strive to complete what the parent tree did not complete.

The terseness of the poems herein takes the reader through a flight marked with reckless abandon only known to lovers who have found true love; one in which two incomplete and compatible beings stumble upon each other even if through "puzzling encounters" to replicate the "birds of paradise". The poems like William Blake's "Tyger", "The Lamb", and others in the *Songs of Innocence and Experience* build on rhetorical questioning. Sue questions the whereabouts of a dear and loved one. This quest takes the reader through the familiar, secluded one-on-one, eye-to-eye encounter and bedroom experiences to unfamiliar crowded bars in search of the familiar yielding yet, incomplete satisfaction. It is the poet's contention that in love, the heart can only remain in love to the extent of its tolerance to be solitary. The poet seems to suggest, in spite of the proverbial, "out of sight is not out of mind" that whenever a heart starts to accumulate inches of dust from abandonment, it is time to move on.

The poems challenge and draw attention to the enormous sacrifices individuals in different professions and walks of life make to take care of people with whom they have nothing in common; as in the poem "nursing". Even in "carte blanche" she evokes these sacrifices to save life as done at the risk and peril of the person striving to save life. This is the poet's call to humanity to watch out for each other; a practice that would make the world a wonderful place in which to live. As if this call were not enough, the poet does not hesitate to remind the reader of the ephemerality of human contacts and the difficulty of mending, through any form of massaging or nurturing by human hands, hearts broken by law. Through other poems, "catch and release" for example, the poet expertly and vividly brings to life the impermanence of human relationships. Also brought to the fore is the indelible nature of the memories of human encounters; happy or painful.

This collection replete with imagery, personification, metaphors, irony, rhetorical questions, polyphony, allusions, etc. displays both mystery and sophistry of human love-hate relationships; at times celebrating love, at times showing the downside of love. It would be erroneous to limit the thematic sweep of this collection which goes way beyond the aforementioned celebration of love-hate to that of lust, loss, separation, transcendence, transience, the endlessness of the cycle of life, and the chastisement of violence and hate. The poet does not abstain from broaching the contemporary themes of fake news, alternate facts, virtual reality, which she uses as an excuse to warn unwitting readers who might be tempted to embrace look-alikes for the real deal.

The greatest celebration the collection showcases is that of the strength of blackness to divert attention from centuries of hurt blacks have endured through enslavement, colonization, neo-colonization, summary execution and elimination of blacks and their leaders. Sue does this by unveiling the pain of the past, which poets past and present have done; but the captivating twist in hers is the imagery of black hurt as a storyteller, cartographer, and memory stimulant. Jogging the perception of the reader, the poet presents and compares bruises and hurt blacks have endured to material things that others gleefully amass. Not only is black pain and hurt invisible, it is the only thing that no matter how much one were to stockpile, it would never get them rich. All in all, the black skin becomes a tableau of hurtful memories "Best buried and forgotten/Leaving behind skin so beautifully scarred" and whose scars are markers of beauty. "carte blanche" tones the hopeful note for the collection: "we spoke of experiences coloured by the darkness of our skins /and whispered dreams for a tomorrow free of present shadows".

The universal appeal of this collection's themes, the poems' terseness, and their overall lyricism are captivating beyond measure and calls for their consumption without moderation.

Bill F. Ndi
poet, playwright, storyteller, critic,
bidirectional English/French translator
Professor of Modern Languages, Communication, and
Philosophy at Tuskegee University, AL, USA.

Part One

birds of paradise

Let's fly away together,
Black wings stretched
O'er the wind beneath
Catch the gleam of the golden hour

Let's chase the sun,
Take a nosedive into the horizon
Figure eights
Eternal loop

With carefree abandon,
And guileless smiles.

puzzling encounters

She hides her face
Beneath the trees
Playing hide and seek
With shadow and light

Living in the both and

Sometimes, she's an ocean
Gushing with secret truths

At others, arid and
segmented
Full of porous vacuums

Begging to be put together

where are you?

Where are you?
You looked me dead in the eyes, And said you'd be back.

Where are you?
I don't feel the familiar weight
Of your body next to mine.
Your broad palm
Is not cupping my left breast,
And the gentle arch of your body is not surrounding mine.

Where are you?
I'm by myself in this crowded bar.
And even with the lights so dim,
I can see clearly that none of these people are you.
Because you see,
I have your features etched in my mind
With a bold bright marker
And even with my eyes closed,
I could tell you apart from a sea of people.

Where are you?
I don't have the answer to that,
But I know where you're not.
You're not there to pick up when I call
At random times because I miss the sound of your voice.
You're not there when life humbles me
And I need someone to catch the tears as they fall
And even on the rare occasion that life brings me joy
You still are nowhere to be found.

I have housed you for too long in my mind

And now the abode I carved
Is gathering inches of dust.
I guess it's time for a spring clean.

So here's to hoping that months down the line
When I've erased you,
You respect me enough not to come in with the
"Hey girl, I miss you."

nursing

I am no one's mother
And yet many, many, many men
Have nursed at my bosom
Taking from me
Things to which they had no right

cpr

I made a mistake,
forgot the rule of impermanence,
forgot forever is a myth.

Now, each string is stretched
taut
throbbing
with the painful memory of what is no more,
can be no more.

Now, I seek relief.

I want the sweet soothing feel of a healing balm
massaged gently between warm, nurturing palms
and rubbed into my ailing heart.

catch and release

I've been held in the palm of many hands.

And if I close my eyes,
I can still trace the lines
Across each broad palm
That cupped me between its calluses.

With time,
Those very hands that formed my cradle
Stretched out ever so slowly
Lifting me up
Only to tilt
me to the side
And dust
me off
like unwanted crumbs.

carte blanche

she was petite, brown,
with
a beautiful mane of unruly dark curls.

we spoke of experiences coloured by the darkness of our skins
and whispered dreams for a tomorrow free of present shadows

she saved lives
but
showed me the scars on her arm which told the tale
of
every time she nearly lost hers

i admired her bravery
she was after all still here on this earth (the ghetto).

then, out of the blue,
she stood up and led me by the hand away from the crowd and
into seclusion.

together,
we turned the key unlocking a part of me
which i was only vaguely aware of before then

she felt soft, smelt like sugar, spice, all things nice and left a
tangy sweetness on my lips.
i melted into her, opening up, giving her carte blanche to my
body

moments later, both sated,

we walked out rejoined the crowd and sang badly to Maroon 5's *She Will Be Loved*.

sweet, sweet loving

My lips are soft and full
They have kissed mounded breasts
Teased tight nipples
And grazed the skin
Of my lovers over the years

They have fixed themselves
To whisper the sweetest nothings
Into the ears of soft warm bodies

My hands, somewhat callused
Have stroked
Gently, forcefully
Leaving trails of pleasure
And coaxing deep, long moans

The generosity of my thighs is unparalleled
And between them flows
The greatest love of all

pas de deux

We danced and twirled in a perfect storm,
my perfect storm.

Each gust of wind whistled in symphony
and when it caught the light,
its beauty was unparalleled.

But slowly,
the storm lost its charm
the dance lost its twirl
perfect wind turned to wild cacophony
and I was left with the chaos of stillness.

The debris fell at my feet
and no longer propelled by the wind,

I sunk into the carnage.

janye

We've had a wonderful journey you and I
Drawing a map to our love.

We took the scenic route
Peeling back layer after layer
To reveal skin so gloriously warm

Being exposed
Has never felt so safe

I see the fullness of your person
And I revel
Sated, content
And beaming with pride

Part Two

lost fruit

The apple doesn't fall far from the tree
And yet
I chafed my skin as I
Plucked myself away from its branches
Unsure if I would survive
Away from this familiar life source
Yet certain I would wither and die still in it
And so
I fell
Propelling myself
So far from the tree as could muster
Looking back
Once or twice
Wishing I could reattach myself
And realizing then with wistful awe
That the separation had healed my wounded flesh
I wondered then if the mighty trunk from whence I came
Would ever notice the absence of the familiar weight
That marked my presence on its branches.

transcendence

The mind can be altered
synapses of the brain rerouted,
Leaving one afloat
On a course, harness only loosely grasped.

I ride it and feel alive.
In only silence.
I have control
Wading this is body, I feel at home.

I touch the colours of my being.
I taste the sounds within my breath.
I glimpse the thoughts that roam free in my head.

I see it all.

I am me,
I am within,
I am without.
I am at peace.

I have broken
past myself.
And I transcend.

passing

Grey cloud
Lightly dense,
Sparse,
Floating through dusk.
Colour descends,
vertical rainbow
Pink, blue, orange
Sink to the ground
To rise another day
This time in reverse
Orange, blue, pink
Circle of colour,
Returning one by one.

Succession. Death. Rebirth

have you eaten?

I come from a long lineage
of proud and brave heroes.

Stories of their greatness
werepassed from father to child
with the cycle repeated
when the child became man.

His was the mantle of keeping the stories
alive in memory.

All this is untrue.

Well, not exactly.
It could very well be,
but I would not know.

You see ours was not a love
which had me seated below
little arms wrapped around their calves
and head perched on their laps
waiting to be regaled with oral histories spanning generations.

Ours was a
'Have you eaten?' kind of love.
The kind which left my fees paid, stomach full and my body
clothed.

Ours was a love that
made sure there was a roof above my head
and it did not leak.

Ours was a love of needs met
where 'I Love Yous' went unsaid.
One that pushed me into the cold embrace of excellence
and kept tabs on my progress from afar.

life, interrupted

How do you say goodbye
To one you are yet to meet?
A gender-less, form-less being,
Care-less-ly, fault-less-ly brought to existence.
How do you exert your right to selfishness
Over one incapable of thought,
Incapable of word,
Incapable of deed?
How do you divest yourself
From its best interests?
How do you evict it from your body,
Your heart, your mind?
How do you tell it you're sorry,
That now is not its time?
How do you stop from feeling guilty?
How do you mourn the loss of what never was?

Part Three

eternity

It's a wonder life goes on
One would think
The volume of my | your | our pain
Would be loud enough
To bring it to a standstill

untitled

pain demands to be felt
to deny it is
to deny yourself and
the healing that follows.

solitaire

There is no company in grief
No one but me
To hold the memories

I am arrested by the fear of forgetting
Lying in wait
As one by one, my senses lose
every recollection of you

Yet, even after scents are lost
And likeness blurred,
My heart is the last muscle holding on
Each beat sends an influx of memory
Laced with all the hurt
That makes grieving far from simple

The heart loves to remember

black strength is finite

i've always thought micro-aggressions
to be a terrible misnomer

there is nothing micro about their violence

and just because
i do not bruise
or balk
or cringe
or cower
or flinch
or quail
or whimper
or wince
at the sound of your words
does not mean
i can endure them incessantly and without reprieve

haine

hate has such a familiar face.
i look in the mirror and
it stares back taunting,
daring me to love myself

lost particles

The million and one atoms
That make up my being,
Have seeped through my pores
And left me for dead.

But what does it matter anyway?

My appetite for this world's antics
Left me so very long ago…

some days

Some days
I walk this life
With a noose in hand
Desperate for the nothingness
The end could bring

beware

Do not mistake puckered lips for kisses

Sometimes, they are merely getting ready to
siphon your essence and leave you on empty.

bruises

I have bruises
Big blue, red and yellow splotches
Battered across my body
Each abrasion is an orator
With a story to tell
Each lesion maps the hurt
Across the undulating terrain of my body
And the sting of the memory they carry
Lingers long after they have lost their colour

Yet veiled by the darkness of my black skin
They draw no attention
Shrouded by the splendour of my sun-kissed sheen
They garner no sympathy
I amass bruise after bruise
And yet I don't feel rich

This black body houses a wealth of hurt
And the evidence is invisible to most.

thank you?

Have you ever been forsaken by gratitude?
It is a thankless place to be.

everyone suffers

I've seen pain
It's etched in the lines across hardened faces
Hollowed eyes and sunken cheeks
It's in the morning rituals of tent packing
And the daily pounding of pavements

Pain is hunger and only
pain satiates pain

I know pain
I accessed it through memory
Guided it in with the intimacy of a long-lost lover
And contorted my body
So it fits in each of my crevices
As an antidote to indifference

I know pain because I know feeling
I know feeling because I know pain.

If I lost my pain,
Would I grieve?

quiltwork

Pieces
Given
Freely
Given
Unknowingly
Given
Unwittingly
Given,
And never returned
Given,
And gone unacknowledged
Leaving fragments Incomplete
Fraying at the hem.

Now we must begin
Sewing
A patchwork quilt
With threadbare pieces
To the fabric of life.

freefall

I was never very good at holding back tears.

These days, I no longer bother.
My cheeks have grown
accustomed to the hot,
salty droplets
that tumble
down,
heralding
release and
healing.

Part Four

home

I'm not meant to,
But I feel at home
In this black skin stretched
across pink flesh covering white bones.

I have made sense
Of the disarray of puzzle pieces in my mind.
Still erratic,
My beating heart brings me comfort.
I wade, floating
In my tsunami of emotions
And I do not drown.

untitled

I refuse to tempt fate
choking on all the shit
life throws
in search of sweetness.

bone apple tea

I want an appetite for life
so voracious
it puts
the gluttony of capitalism to shame.

petite fille

Little girl
Promise me
You'll return to that wide toothy grin
Swear to me
You'll leap again
With that spring in your step
Give me your word
Cross your heart
And hope to die

journeying

I know a longer way home,
Ways back that can take forever
Just follow the yellow brick road
Then go down
Into the rabbit hole
Don't be afraid of the darkness
Just freefall
Until you find your light.

amor sui

I etch my calloused hands
across facial features,
and familiar hate
softens to love.

someday

Someday soon
The time will come
When my world
Will turn on its axis
Bandaging along the way
All the fissures
From life's earthquakes, trembles and tremors

Someday soon
The time will come
When my body
Will shed
Memories
Best left forgotten
Leaving behind skin so beautifully scarred

Someday soon, someday
That time shall come.

(temporary) elation

Savour joy.
Let its sweetness
Seep into your tastebuds
And wash away
The acrid bitterness of sadness past.
Do a little jiggle
And feel your muscles
Lose the tension
Of wound up anxiety.
And when the taste is spent,
Have a little faith.
It will be back
Much sooner than you think.

ever green

In my mind
I am evergreen
Tall and rooted
Floating in the clouds
with reckless abandon.

Ehb

Beneath the golden star
Closed eyes
Orange glow
Permeates

Hot rays seep
Below the dermis
Trickle with intensity
Towards centre

Warm wind envelops
Brushing skin gently

Fractured being
Fused in stillness
By elemental forces.